Martha Washington's Big Day

Author **Barbie Marie**
Illustrated by **Terry Honstead**

First Lady Press

www.barbaraschlichting.com

The East River was three blocks away so the streets were very busy with carriages, animals, and street vendors because of the arrival of ships along the riverfront. Crowds of people followed her brigade to the Presidential house to get a glimpse of the President's wife.

"We've arrived," Lady Washington said to her adopted two grandchildren, Nelly and Wash. (Short for Washington).

My name is Gloria. I am the rag doll in Itty's pocket (Unbeknownst to Itty, Gloria understood everything that was said, and she told stories to her doll friends in the evening when the household was asleep).

Through my eyes, Mrs. Washington looked nice and friendly. She was short and plump, with a twinkle in her eye. President Washington was delighted to see her. The couple were complete opposites in size and shape, but when he leaned over and whispered in her ear, she giggled.

"What a lovely house, George," Mrs. Washington said, entering the house. "It's a fine brick building and a 'handsomely furnished house.'"

First Lady Mrs. Washington barely had time to greet her husband because of the throngs of people who followed her into the house.

From Thursday morning on, I was always tucked inside of Itty's pocket. It made me accessible to all matters concerning Lady Washington. Lady Washington barely had time to settle in because of all the well-wishers who came to meet her and the President.

Itty didn't have her ears covered, so I didn't either. We heard President and Lady Washington discussing the role of First Lady.

"Why am I not allowed to invite my friends for tea or sewing?" Lady Washington asked.

"We cannot show favoritism. Thursday evening's we will host dinner parties. The guest list will be politically balanced," Mr. Washington said.

"What else do I need to know?"

"Friday evening, beginning tomorrow night, you will host a reception. When Congress is in session, you will have guests."

"When will I be allowed to visit with my friends?"

"Only certain individuals are invited here. We must be non-partisan."
Itty stood when her lady left the room and entered the hallway.

Lady Washington asked for tea. Itty placed me near a pillow where I observed my lady. After catching up on correspondence, she reached for her knitting bag. She knitted warm woolen socks.

"Here is your tea," Itty said. She set the tray with tea and biscuits down. "Who are the socks for?"

"There are plenty of people in need after the war," Lady Washington replied.

On Friday, the household bustled with guests. Lady Washington barely had a moment before she had to get ready for the evening's reception.

"Tonight is my first reception," Lady Washington said. "Itty, will you make sure that the children are entertained? I fear it'll be a long evening."

"Yes Lady Washington," Itty said.

Washington picked up her quilt square from a basket and began studying it. I noticed that she'd painstakingly cut blocks to a certain measurement. She held one up high for me to see.

Suddenly, she winked and smiled at me! Just as quick, she tapped my nose!

I watched with reverence from that moment on as she pieced together the rose quilt block. When morning came to a close and she was summoned to entertain more unknown guests, she picked me up and carried me along.

I was picked up by one of Abigail Adams' grandchildren and carried away. I wondered what would become of me?

What will become of Gloria…find out in the next book….

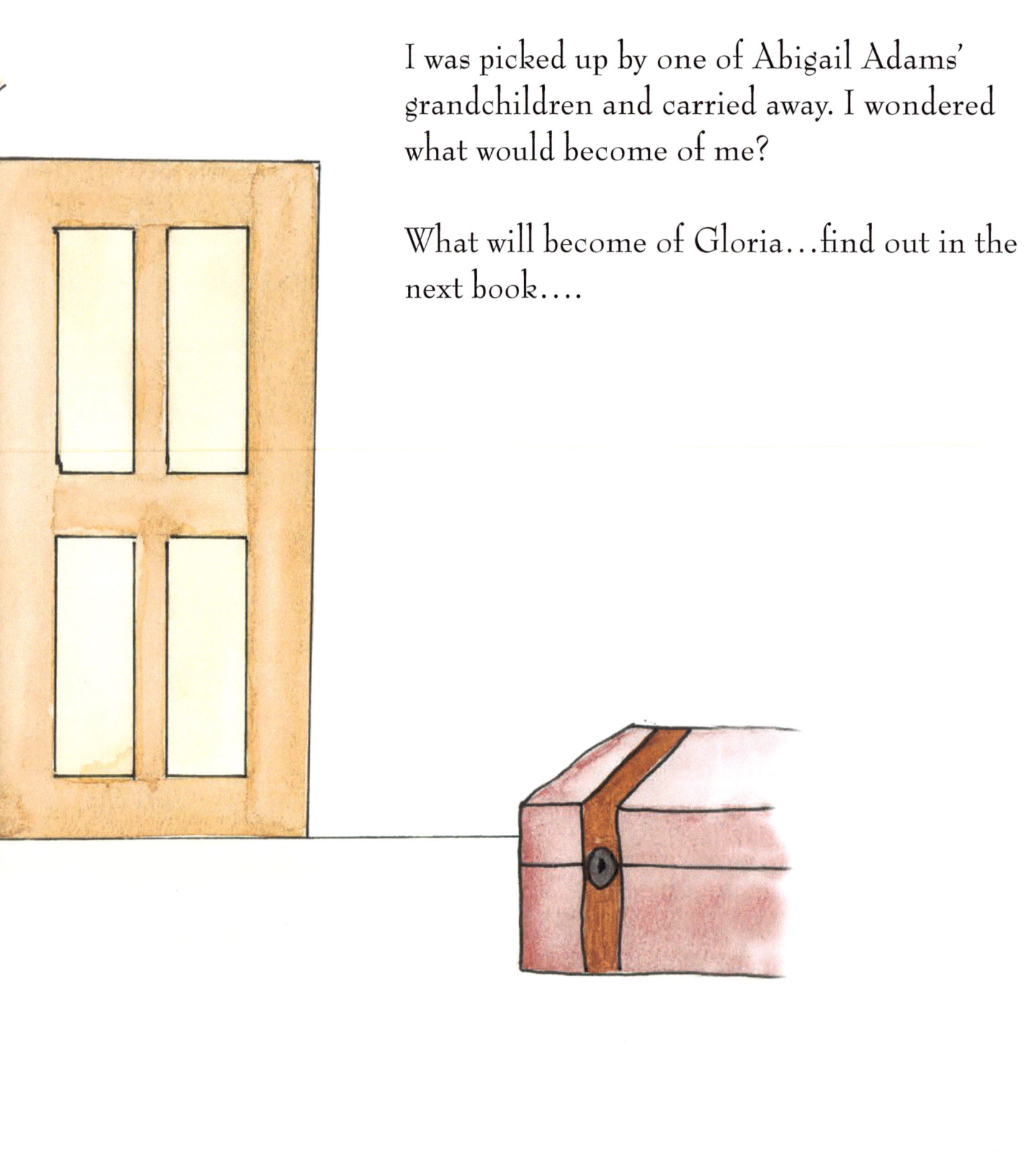

First Lady Martha Washington supported her husband until he resigned from his second term in office. Both looked forward to retirement from public life. In those days, Martha Washington's title was Lady. She'd been widowed and owned property before marrying Mr. Washington. The government nor the citizens knew what to call the President or his wife. They didn't want king or queen. President and Mrs. President or Mrs. Presidentress were common titles at the time.

The capital in Philadelphia was better to her liking because it was his second term and as First Lady, she was allowed to choose her guests and had more control over official dinners and receptions.

First Ladies Mystery Series

Dolley Madison: THE BLOOD SPANGLED BANNER

Mary Lincoln: IF WORDS COULD KILL

Edith Wilson: THE CLUE OF THE DANCING BELL

Edith Wilson: FOURTEEN POINTS to DEATH

A WHITE HOUSE DOLLHOUSE MYSTERY

HISTORICAL FICTION

BODY ON THE TRACKS

www.barbaraschlichting.com.